HAIRCUTS ARE NO BIG DEAL

BY

ASHLEY VERCAMMEN

ILLUSTRATED BY PUTUT PUTRI

Haircuts are No Big Deal 2023 © 2023 by Ashley Vercammen. All rights reserved.

Published by Home Style Teachers. www.ashley-vercammen.ca.

All rights reserved. This book contains material protected under international and federal copyright laws and treaties. Any unauthorized reprint or use of this material is prohibited. No part of this book may be reproduced or transmitted in any form or by any means, electronic or mechanical, including photocopying, recording, or by any information storage and retrieval system without express written permission from the author.

Identifier: ISBN: 978-1-77815-295-5 (paperback)

"Today's the day!" Charlie yelled. "I will get my hair cut, and it's no big deal."

"That's right," said mom. "Just like we practiced. First, you get your hair cut and then"...

" I get my prize," Charlie cheered.

"Now remember," said mom, "when we open the door, the bell will ring. You don't have to worry though because it's"...

" no big deal!" Charlie cheered.

"I will help you hang your jacket. We will be back for it before we go home". Said mom.

Charlie likes to wear his jacket, but he can't wear it during the haircut, or it will be itchy.

"Next, you will sit in the big chair with some of your favourite toys, snacks, and shows," mom says with a smile.

"Do you remember meeting Emma? She will be there to cut your hair".

"Next, we will put this cape around your neck. You will wear this for the timer, just like we practiced". Mom said as she pulled up his chair.

"We will keep it nice and loose around your neck, just like this!" Mom held up his red cape.
Charlie groaned. "It may be a bit tight too".

"It is only for the timer," mom said. "You can do it because..."
"it's no big deal," Charlie cheered!
"That's right," Mom said.

"She is very nice! Will you be there too, mommy?" Charlie asked, knowing the answer.

"Of course, I will be there too," she smiled.
"There might be a big mirror in front of the chair, but we can cover it with something fun or make funny faces together," Mom said.

"Let's practice. First, we put on the cape, then we can pick a show to watch," said mom.

"Can I pick the show?" Charlie asked excitedly. "Of course!" Said mom. "Let's think of some while we wait for our turn!"

"I will bring our timer from home, and you will hear the sound for 2 minutes while Emma cuts your hair with a shaver. But we don't have to worry." mom said.

"It's no big deal!" Charlie cheered.

"That's right, let's practice again! When the timer goes off, you get to have a break to play." Said mom excitedly.

"Ok, I set the timer. I love how you are being so brave." Mom said calmly as she tickled Charlie.

"Mom, it's no big deal," said Charlie. "You're right, and I will be there the whole time, just in case you need to pause for a break," Mom assured Charlie.

"First, Emma will use the scissors during the timer, and then you get a break!" mom told Charlie.

"Can we go to the park?!" he asked excitedly.

"Not this time, but we can read a book or play with cars together." She said eagerly.

"Ok!" Charlie yelled. "I will bring Marty, my favourite truck."

"When our break is over, we will start the timer again," Mom told Charlie.

"First, Emma will use the shaver for the timer, and then you will get another break!"

"Let's practice. You will hear the shaver and feel it on your neck." Mom said calmly.

"Here we go! Emma will touch your ears with the shaver, and it's..." "no big deal," Charlie cheered.

Mom smiled "she will touch your neck with the shaver, and it's..." "no big deal," Charlie giggled.

"That's right!" mom said proudly. "She will touch your head alllll around, and it's...."
"it's no big deal," Charlie said, copying mom proudly.

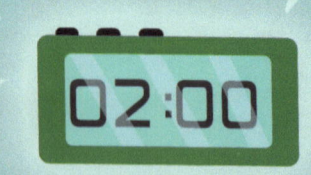

Mom and Charlie went to the barber.
"Off we go. I hear the bell." Said mom.

"Hello, Emma!" Charlie said as he looked for his cars.

"Hi Charlie, check it out! I have your chair with some cool cars ready to go!" Emma said excitedly.

30 minutes later...

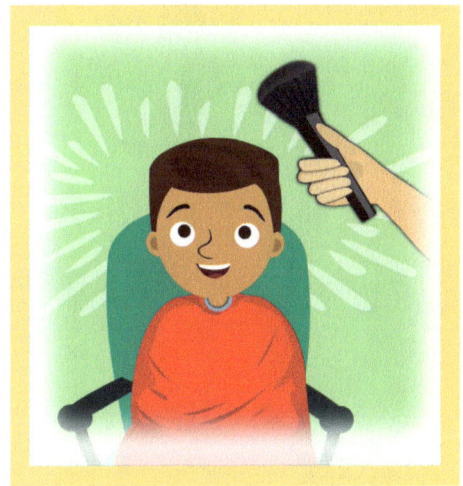

"Ta Da!" sang Emma.

"You got your hair cut and sat so still!" Mom smiled. "You were really brave when you heard all of the sounds," Mom said as she squeezed Charlie tightly.

"Trying new things can be scary sometimes, but when we practice, mom paused.

"it's no big deal!!" Charlie yelled.

"See you later Emma" Charlie said with a wave!

No Big Deals

Hey there, friend! Do you ever feel nervous or scared about doing things like getting a haircut or going to the dentist? It's totally normal to feel that way, but it's important to practice those tricky self-care tasks so we can take good care of ourselves.

One way to practice is by starting with "No Big Deals." Getting a haircut can be a big deal for many people. If sitting in a chair is "No Big Deal" then that is a great place to start! By breaking these big skills down into smaller skills, we can celebrate each step until things like haircuts become "No Big Deal." This takes time, though! So the key is to practice!

Remember, it's okay to feel scared or nervous sometimes, but we don't want those feelings to stop us from taking care of ourselves. By practicing these steps, we can overcome those tricky tasks and feel proud of ourselves for taking care of our bodies and minds. Keep up the good work!

Strategies for No Big Deals

- Practice, Practice, Practice!
- Use visual timers or tokens to make expectations clear.
- Allow for frequent breaks to keep everyone successful.
- Use "first", "then" statements and keep things **positive**!
    - "First sit in the chair, then we can choose your show!"

www.ingramcontent.com/pod-product-compliance
Lightning Source LLC
Chambersburg PA
CBHW042027150426
43198CB00002B/91